YOUR

Discover Your

Empowering Purpose

Live Your Life with More Meaning,

Significance and Fulfillment

Michael E. Angier

Published by Success Networks International, Inc.
Tampa Bay, Florida 34609-9509
www.SuccessNet.org

ISBN: 9781076439307

Professional Reviews

"It always amazes me, considering this is the stuff I write about, that I can consistently pick up a book by Michael Angier and be inspired yet again. His clear understanding and easy manner of communication always deliver a message deep into the heart, breaking through barriers and waking us up. Another must read from Michael. Bravo!"

—Dr. Steve Taubman
www.SteveTaubman.com

"This whole series is pure gold. I love the way Michael challenges us to live our best lives with real authenticity. Everyone can benefit from the clarity this book provides."

—Susan McGrogan
www.CodingServicesGroup.com

"This book makes the process of discovering your purpose come alive. In an easy-to-read format, filled with potent quotes, practical exercises, and personal insight, you are introduced to powerful tools which will assist you in your journey. Whether you already know your purpose—and want to confirm or clarify it—or desire to discover your purpose, you will be well served within these pages. An excellent read created by a person who has spent his life helping people live their Best Lives."

—Steve Ulrich
www.PathToClarity.com

Table of Contents

Introduction

"Your purpose in life is to find your purpose and give your whole heart and soul to it."

—Buddha

I wrote this book to help you discover your own Empowering Purpose for your life and the reasons why. This book (and the entire *Your Best Life* series) is dedicated to helping you live your very best life (see Chapter One for Best Life definition).

What is Your Purpose?

Your purpose is not a goal to be achieved, and it's not the fulfillment of a picture you've created for yourself (see my book on *How to Create a Vivid Vision for Your Life*).

It's a calling—more like a direction than an objective—and one that may very well never be fulfilled. Although you will surely find its pursuit to be very fulfilling.

Why Does Your Purpose Matter?

I'll explain more about this in Chapter Two, but for now, let me just borrow some words from fellow author Steve Goodier: "Not everybody will identify a purpose in life. But when you do, and when you pursue it, you will be living the kind of life you feel you were meant to live. And what's more, you will be happy."

Michael E. Angier

Having a clear purpose adds meaning to your life that creates fulfillment, joy and significance. When you are clear on your purpose and committed to its pursuit, I guarantee you a richer, more rewarding and gratifying life—and with less struggle.

Never Too Old

Many people will think they are too old to discover their Empowering Purpose for their life. That's just not true.

Having a clear purpose earlier in your life might have been better, but no one can change the past—not even God!

Whether you are 22 or 82, it's never too late to work through the process I will set forth for you. No one knows how much time they have left on this planet. Clarity on your purpose and conviction in its pursuit will make the rest of your life the best of your life. It will put life in your years and not simply years in your life.

Perhaps Dr. Wayne Dyer said it best: "Don't die with your music still in you. Don't die with your purpose unfulfilled. Don't die feeling as if your life has been wrong. Don't let that happen to you."

> *"Don't die with your music still in you. Don't die with your purpose un-fulfilled. Don't die feeling as if your life has been wrong. Don't let that happen to you."*
> —Dr. Wayne Dyer

Two Most Important Days of Your Life

Mark Twain is most often credited with saying, "The two most important days in your life are the day you are born and the day you figure out why." It was true over 100 years ago and it's still true today.

> *"The two most important days in your life are the day you are born and the day you figure out why."*
> —Mark Twain

Are you excited to discover your purpose—or deepen the one you think you have? I am. Let's get to it.

Michael E. Angier

This Book is for You if . . .

"I went to the woods because I wished to live deliberately, to front only the essential facts of life, and see if I could not learn what it had to teach, and not, when I came to die, discover that I had not lived."
—Henry David Thoreau

This book is for anyone who feels they are unsure or unaware of their purpose in life. If you are looking for more meaning, more significance or a stronger why to your existence, you will find great help and substantial reward in reading and applying what this book recommends.

If you haven't got any idea what your purpose is, this will guide you to discover your purpose. If you have a sense of your purpose, but would like to deepen and enrich your purpose, it will also help you.

If you'd like to help others discover their own Empowering Purpose, you will find great insights into how to do that.

If you would like to create a Vivid Vision and a Meaningful Mission for your life, you can do so with an Empowering Purpose as your solid foundation.

Michael E. Angier

In doing so, you will live your best life with few to no regrets and capture all the richness, the fullness and the abundance that life has to offer. You will have more conviction, more reasons and more passion. And it will carry you through the challenging times and difficult obstacles that will inevitably be found in your path. You can create a big life, and having an Empowering Purpose makes it much bigger yet.

While most people "live lives of quiet desperation," you will march forth with a commitment and confidence few people can even imagine.

Chapter 1
Your Best Life

"Decide what kind of life you really want . . . And then, say no to everything that isn't that."

Are You Seeking Your Best Life?

Before we get into the nitty gritty of discovering your Empowering Purpose, let's take a look at our objectives.

If you're reading this, I assume you want a better life. You want to improve on where you are. Maybe a little. Maybe a lot.

Regardless of where you find yourself at this point in time—and regardless of your age—you can certainly improve. After all, the biggest room in the world is the room for improvement.

You may be wanting to take your on-purpose, comfortable life and simply make it better. Or maybe your life is a train wreck.

Either way, you have to start with the end in mind.

It's important to acknowledge where you are, but there will be plenty of time for that. What's more important is getting clear on where you're going.

Michael E. Angier

Your best life doesn't just happen. It doesn't automatically unfold, and it's certainly not handed to you. You have to design and create your best life yourself. Because if you don't, other people and outside circumstances will do it for you. And do you know what other people and outside circumstances have planned for you? Hardly anything at all.

What Does Your Best Life Look Like?

No doubt you have some idea about what your Best Life looks like. I assume you have some goals—some things you want to accomplish or experience before you make your departure from planet Earth.

Have you ever envisioned in great detail how you would like to have your life unfold? Do you see it? Can you taste it? Do you believe it?

The clearer you can become on all the things you want in your life—and the reasons why—the easier it will be to do what you need to do to achieve them.

We all want to be happy, and I personally believe we are happiest when we are in pursuit of our highest and best.

For now, let me share with you, in general terms, what I mean by your Best Life. It should give you some seminal ideas for your Best Life Plan.

*"Your Best Life is a life
with no regrets."*

It's a tall order, but I think your Best Life is a life without regrets.

Your Best Life is a life by design—not default.

I think you should build a life from which you don't need a vacation. Not that you won't *take* vacations, but you won't *need* them. Because your vocation will be your avocation. And it's not a struggle; it's a wiggle.

"Your Best Life requires your best self."

Your Best Life requires your best self. If you want your life to get better, *you* have to get better. I'm guessing that's why you're reading this book.

For me it means rising to a calling instead of an alarm clock. I get up when I *want* to get up, and I use an alarm clock only once or twice a year. It is possible.

I believe your Best Life is a life of clarity, purpose, passion and prosperity. A life designed around your values, principles and intentions.

Simply put—a life on your terms. You get to design, define, create and live Your Best Life.

Top Seven Results of Living Your Best Life

The following seven benefits are what I consider the biggest payoffs for creating a life well lived.

1. Significance & Meaning

2. Time, Location & Financial Freedom

3. Happiness, Fun & Adventure

4. Purpose & Integrity

5. Confidence & Self-esteem

6. Rich Relationships

7. Health, Fitness & Vitality

Sounds worthwhile, yes?

Your full and unique potential is unknown. But certainly worth going for, don't you think? Who can count the number of apples in a single apple seed?

"Death is not the greatest loss in life. The greatest loss is what dies inside us while we live."

—Norman Cousins

The Path to Your Best Life

The illustration below shows what I believe to be the best path to your best life—however you might define it. The bottom four tiers are foundational. The top three are much more dynamic. But they should stand in support of your core values, purpose, mission and vision.

Tasks
Projects
Goals
Vision
Mission
Purpose
Core Values

The Path to Your Best Life

Anything, Not Everything

My belief is that you can do *anything* in this life. But you can't do *everything*. That's why it's so important to choose your goals, your projects and your tasks wisely. And to base them on the foundational steps of core values, purpose, mission and vision.

> *"You can do* anything *you want in this life. You just can't do* everything *you want."*

Otherwise, you're making choices and spending your precious time and energy on your own or others' whims.

Michael E. Angier

The first foundational step (Core Values) is not within the scope of this book, but I strongly encourage you to think carefully about them. Getting clear on your core values, your purpose and your mission, will help you to avoid regrets and feel like you invested your life in the best way possible.

Although you can uncover your Empowering Purpose without a clear sense of your most important core values, you will find it easier, and most likely a much more empowering and effective Purpose, if you know your top core values. SuccessNet has an inexpensive course you can use to go through this process. It's a home-study course that's available in print form as well as an online video course at no additional cost. You can access a discounted price on the Your Core Values Course at www.Your-CoreValues.com

---

"Life should not be a journey to the grave with the intention of arriving safely in a pretty and well-preserved body, but rather to skid in broadside in a cloud of smoke, thoroughly used up, totally worn out, and loudly proclaiming 'Wow, what a ride!' "
—Hunter S. Thompson

The bottom line is that unless you invest the time, energy and money in creating a life you truly want, you're going to be spending a lot of time and effort supporting a life you *don't* want.

"Unless you invest the time, energy and money in creating a life you truly want, you're going to be spending a lot of time and effort supporting a life you don't want.*"*
—Michael E. Angier

Action Steps

Consider this engaging and inspiring home-study and video course on discovering and clarifying your core values. To find out more, go to www.YourCoreValues.com

Thousands of people have taken this course and benefited greatly from the process.

Michael E. Angier

Chapter 2
The Trouble with Not Having Purpose

"Unless you focus on what you want,
you will spend the rest of your life
focusing on what others want you to
focus on."

—Moe Nawaz

OK, so you're reading a book about discovering your Empowering Purpose. And you've made it this far. Good for you.

You're probably thinking that you're pretty well sold on the value of this process and how you will live the life of your dreams.

But I ask you to take one more step with me.

What's a life *without* an Empowering Purpose? Why does that suck?

Think about it. Most people do not have a clear purpose. They spend more time planning their family vacations than they do planning their Best Life.

Michael E. Angier

Look around. Most people's life is far less than great. Even the ones who seem to have it together—have good jobs, make decent money, etc.—have far less success and happiness than they are capable of having.

Several studies in recent years here in the United States report that only about half of the people surveyed consider themselves happy—only *half*. And I would submit that less than half of *those* "happy" people would say they are living to their full and unique potential.

Let's face it, most people simply drift through life taking what comes, complaining about it and surrendering to "The Rat Race." Maybe a goal here or a goal there, but mostly just drifting.

They lack the planning, the belief, the confidence and the commitment to being a "10" on the Go-For-It Scale. As Henry David Thoreau wrote: "The mass of men lead lives of quiet desperation. What is called resignation is confirmed desperation."

Life without a plan—life without purpose—is a waste.

On a more positive note, see what Thoreau had to say about a more *directed* life. The often-quoted first sentence is probably not new to you. But pay close attention to the rest of the quote and the promise that it offers: "If one advances confidently in the direction of his dreams, and endeavors to live the life which he has imagined, he will meet with a success unexpected in common hours. He will put some things behind, will pass an invisible boundary; new, universal, and more liberal laws will begin to establish themselves around and within him; or old laws will be expanded and interpreted in his favor in a more liberal sense, and he will live with a license of a higher order of beings."

A "license of a higher order of beings". Please take a moment and ponder that. It's pretty weighty stuff.

It sure beats the sucky, unplanned, uninspiring, unimpressive, unhappy, less-than-your-best, live-by-default life, yes?

Action Step

Commit to finishing this book and working through a plan for developing your Empowering Purpose. You are worth it. Your Best Life is worth it.

You can always go back to not having an Empowering Purpose, but please promise yourself you will finish this book and give it a shot.

Michael E. Angier

Chapter 3
Build on Your Strengths

"Each person's greatest room for growth is in the areas of his or her greatest strength."
—Donald O. Clifton,
Now, Discover Your Strengths

Many success gurus advise us to shore up the weak areas of our life—getting better at things we don't do well. I'm all for improving oneself, but I think that approach is misguided. It places your attention on what you *don't* enjoy doing instead of on what you *do* enjoy doing.

I'm confident that you will have more joy and success by focusing on getting better at what you're *already* good at. No doubt you had teachers and perhaps parents who kept calling attention to your weaknesses rather than your strengths. In doing so, it most likely eroded your confidence—at least to some degree. You thought less of yourself because your so-called shortcomings were where your focus was.

We all have things we're good at—and things we *aren't* so good at. We all have certain talents, skills, interests and propensities. And no one is great at everything. So don't concentrate your

19

God-given talents on the things you find hard, challenging and unfulfilling.

It's too big a life to be doing things you don't enjoy—and that you suck at doing.

Albert Einstein said, "Everyone is a genius. But if you judge a fish by its ability to climb a tree, it will live its whole life believing that it is stupid." I think what Einstein stated illustrates quite well the point I'm trying to make. I think it will make a huge difference in you living your best life while following your purpose. If nothing else, you'll have more fun and a lot less stress and disappointment.

"Everyone is a genius. But if you judge a fish by its ability to climb a tree, it will live its whole life believing that it is stupid."
—Albert Einstein

But what if there are life skills you're not good at, but seem important to you in fulfilling your life mission? Hire it done. I'm confident you can make a lot more money pursuing your passions than not. So you can simply pay people to do things *they're* good at. It's a win/win, for sure.

Some of the best advice I ever got was to charge the most for the services I found the easiest to deliver. There were things I had to offer about which I underestimated their value because they came easy to me—and I assumed they were easy for others as well. But that's simply not the case.

Don't denigrate or undervalue what you do simply because it's not hard for you. The value of your product or service has nothing to do with how long it took or how hard it was to produce. The value is in whether it solved a problem or fulfilled a want. Chances are, what you're good at is hard for someone else—and they'll pay you for your talents.

"Focus on Your Strengths . . .
Delegate Your Weaknesses."

What's Your Zone of Genius?

A key step in discovering your Empowering Purpose is knowing your strengths, talents and skills. Why else would you be given these things if it wasn't to affect your purpose?

You certainly don't want to waste your gifts.

By being clear on what makes you feel good, on what's fulfilling, meaningful and significant, you can begin to understand your purpose and execute on your mission.

The following list is to get you thinking about your particular Zone of Genius. I'm sure there are items on the list that you hadn't thought of, and I'm sure you can add some of your own.

I suggest you go through the list and circle the talents and skills that you are good at, highly interested in and/or enjoy doing. Then, go through the circled items and highlight the ones that

Michael E. Angier

you are the best at, passionate about or find great joy in doing. This process will get you closer to honing your Zone of Genius and will lay the foundation for creating an Empowering Purpose and eventually a Meaningful Mission.

Action Step

Download a copy of this Strengths/Talents/Knowledge/Skills List from www.SuccessNet.org/mission/genius.pdf or use the list here in the book to circle and highlight your talents and skills.

You may also want to enlist the help of a trusted friend—someone who knows you well. They may see talents and skills in you that you were not aware of or have not yet appreciated.

Strengths/Talents/Knowledge/Skills List

What am I good at doing? What is my Zone of Genius?

Academics	Asking Questions
Accepting	Assertiveness
Accounting	Athleticism
Acting/Drama	Authentic
Adaptability	Awareness
Adventurous	Baking
Advertising	Big Thinker
Analyzing the Past	Boating
Art	Bookkeeping
Articulate	Brainstorming

Budgeting

Building Things

Calculating/Math

Caring

Carefrontation

Careful/Cautious

Catalyst

Charismatic

Coaching

Collaborative

Complimentary

Communication Skills

Computers/IT

Confident

Conflict Resolution

Considerate

Consistency

Consulting

Cooking

Courteous

Courageous

Copywriting

Creative

Critical Analysis

Critical Thinking

Curiosity

Customer Relationship Management

Dance

Data Analysis

Decision Making

Delegating

Dependable

Designer

Detail Orientation

Determined

Developer

Dexterity

Diplomacy

Discerning

Drawing

Driving

Eager to Grow

Editing

Empathetic

Encouraging Others

Energetic

Engineering

Enthusiasm

Entrepreneurial

Facilitator

Fact Checking

Fairness

Financial Management

Financial Planning

Firm

Fishing

Fitness/Strength

Fixing/Repairing Things

Flexibility

Flying (pilot)

Focused

Foreign Language

Friendly

Future Thinking

Gaming

Gardening

Goal Directed

Generous

Get Along Well with Others

Good Hearted

Good Judgment

Good Manners/Polite

Good Memory

Good Speaker

Good Vocabulary

Good Writer

Good with Tools

Graphic Design

Gregarious

Handle Change

Hardworking

Health/Fitness

High Energy

Hiring/Recruiting

Honest

Human Resources

Humility

Humorous

Identify Strengths and Weaknesses

Imagination

Inclusive

Independent

Industrious

Initiative

Innovation

Inspiring

Integrity/Honesty

Intelligence

Intuition

Inventiveness

Investment Strategies

Jokes/Humor

Joyful

Juggling

Knowledgeable

Leader

Learning

Legal

Listening

Logistics

Loyalty

Magic

Magnanimous

Maintenance/Routine Tasks

Making Connections

Making Friends

Managing Money

Marketing

Martial Arts

Math

Mechanics

Mediator

Meeting Management

Mentorship

Multi-Tasking

Multiple Languages

Music

Narration

Negotiating

Michael E. Angier

Networking (in the virtual world)

Networking (person to person)

Observing

Open Minded

Optimism

Organization

Outgoing

Parenting

Passionate

Patience

People Judgment

People Skills

Performing (drama)

Perseverance

Persistent

Personal Productivity

Persuasive

Photography

Planning

Pleasant Demeanor

Positive Attitude

Practical

Principle-Driven

Prioritizing

Problem Solver

Productivity

Programming

Project Management

Proofing

Public Speaking

Punctuality

Purposeful

Quick-Witted

Raise Money

Reading

Reading People Well

Realistic

Recruiting

Reflective

Relaxation

Reliability

Relieve Stress

Remembering

Reporting

Research

Resilience (ability to deal
with setbacks)

Resourcefulness

Results Oriented

Risk Management

Romantic

Sailing

Sales

Search Engine Optimization

Self-Confidence

Self-Control

Self-Management

Self-Assurance

Self-Discipline

Selling

Sense of Humor

Serious

Shopping

Sign Language

Sincerity

Singing

Smart

Sociable

Social Intelligence

Social Media

Software

Spiritual

Spotting New Trends

Storytelling

Strategic Planning

Stress Management

Sympathetic

Systems Management

Taking Risks

Taxes

Teaching/Training

Team Building

Tending to Plants

Test Taking

Thinking

Thinking Outside the Box

Time Integrity (punctual)

Time Management

Tolerance

Training

Troubleshooting

Trustworthy

Typing

Video Creation

Visionary

Voiceover

Volunteering

Website

Well-Intentioned

Willing to Accept Feedback

Witty

Wisdom

Woodworking

Working with Animals

Works Well Under Pressure

Writing/Authoring

SCOT Analysis

Another exercise that's helpful in getting clearer on your strengths and opportunities is the SCOT process.

SCOT stands for Strengths, Challenges, Opportunities and Threats. You may have heard of it as SWOT, (with the W standing for weaknesses) but I didn't like weaknesses and replaced it with Challenges.

I maintain two ongoing SCOTs. One for my business and one for my life.

What are your **strengths**? What are you good at? What's working in your favor? Experience. Talents. Skills. Savings, etc. Put it all down and add to it over time.

What are your **challenges**? Big or small, list them all. What are the problems you face? Where do you not have an advantage? What causes you to hold back and not go for it? Of course, you will eventually figure out what you can do about these challenges.

What are your **opportunities**? What could you do that's available to you? Remember that you can do *anything*, you just can't do *everything*. You'll need to choose carefully. This is the place to write them all down so you don't lose them.

What are the **threats**? What could become a problem for you? You certainly don't want to *dwell* on threats that could come your way, but you don't want to bury your head in the sand either. Once you know what they are, you can insure, protect or prevent them from causing you harm.

Michael E. Angier

Action Step

Start a SCOT Analysis and keep it where you can update it from time to time. It's very helpful.

Chapter 4
Uncovering Your Purpose

---

*"The purpose of life
is a life of purpose."*
—Robert Byrne

OK, by this time, you probably feel twinges of excitementd about the power of having an Empowering Purpose and can see the benefits of focusing your life with more passion, meaning and significance.

You also should have a good handle on your top talents, skills and interests. You should be getting close to knowing—or already know—your Zone of Genius.

Don't "Push the River"

As I've intimated, your purpose isn't something so much to be created as it is to *discover*. And you've begun to lay the groundwork for that discovery. You may have even realized it already. If not, please be patient. This is not something that you want to force. You may uncover it quickly or it may take a good while.

Stay open, trust the process and believe that your true purpose will be revealed in its own time. It may happen by the time you finish this book or it may come weeks later.

Michael E. Angier

This is important. We're talking about finding your unique purpose—your True North. And this is no time to "push the river." Just live in the question: What's my Empowering Purpose?

That said, I think it's good to write down possible or even likely candidates for your purpose. Start trying some of them on.

Enjoy the Journey

Whether the discovery of your Empowering Purpose happens quickly or takes longer than you expected, be patient. It *will* come. And it will be worth it. I suggest you look upon uncovering your Empowering Purpose as an adventure. Be curious. No doubt you will discover things about yourself that you hadn't before. It's not a test. Play with it. Have fun.

Do You Have it Already?

If you think you are already clear on your purpose, if you think you've already got it, I recommend sitting with it some. Stay open to the idea that there may be something else—something deeper, something bigger, something more compelling. You may have it, and you may not. There's still some questioning left to do.

The power of clarity is not to be underestimated here. When you are clear, what you want in your life shows up. And the quality and quantity of what shows up is in direct proportion to your degree of clarity.

"When you are clear, what you want in your life shows up. And the quality and quantity of what shows up is in direct proportion to your degree of clarity."
—Michael E. Angier

Something that may help you to envision your Empowering Purpose is to look for it in the "sweet spot" that lies at the confluence of the following three areas:

1. Your Interests and Passions

2. Your Skills, Talents and Knowledge

3. Your Core Values

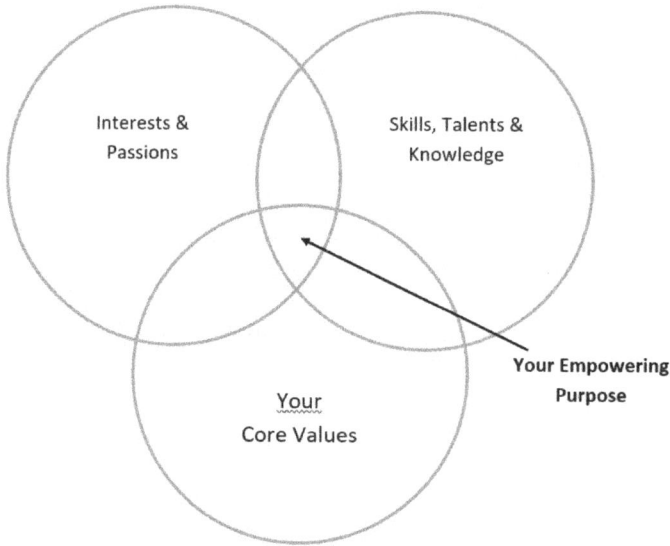

Interests & Passions

Skills, Talents & Knowledge

Your Core Values

Your Empowering Purpose

Action Steps

Start a journal entry, a notebook or a computer file of possible candidates for your Empowering Purpose.

And be sure to congratulate yourself for taking on this awesome project. Your courage and commitment have lifted you far above the many who drift through life with little or no purpose.

Chapter 5
My Purpose is . . .

---

*"There is one quality which
one must possess to win, and
that is definiteness of purpose,
the knowledge of what one
wants, and a burning desire to
possess it."*

—Napoleon Hill
Think & Grow Rich

Your ideal Empowering Purpose is a clear, concise statement with meaning and conviction. It's your reason for being, or as the French say, your "raison d'être".

A personal purpose statement defines who you are. It reflects your passions and core values.

It's the answer to the proverbial question, "Why am I here?"

You might start with some sentence completions such as:

My purpose is . . .

The reason I'm here is to . . .

My reason for being is to . . .

I make a difference in the world by . . .

Michael E. Angier

I was born to . . .

I encourage you to write anything that comes to mind. No one else needs to see your first attempts at defining your Empowering Purpose. This is not a time to limit yourself in any way. Nothing is too big or too grandiose. No judgment.

Just like brainstorming, any idea can stimulate a great idea. You are brainstorming with yourself in search of your magnum opus.

Refining Your Statement

Your Empowering Purpose statement is a work in progress. Sometimes when you work on it, words will flow easily. Other times, not so much. The important thing is to let it flow, let it unfold and evolve. It will come.

What you authentically and consistently seek, you will surely find.

> *What you authentically and consistently seek,*
> *you will surely find.*

Write in the Present Tense

"I am." "I do." Not "I will." Present tense is empowering. It's here. It's now—a reflection of who you are in the world—right now.

Examples

Here are a few examples of personal purpose statements. Please use them to stimulate ideas rather than copy them.

"To evoke the greatness in those I meet. To live as an instrument for divine possibilities."

"To be a loving teacher of simple truths to help myself and others to awaken the presence of God in their lives."

"I'm a teacher. I help people bring out the best in themselves and in their organizations."

"To serve as a leader, live a balanced life, and apply ethical principles to make a significant difference."

"To be a teacher. And to be known for inspiring my students to be more than they thought they could be."

"To have fun in [my] journey through life and learn from [my] mistakes."

"To use my gifts of intelligence, charisma, and serial optimism to cultivate the self-worth and net-worth of women around the world."

"To be a gentle force for comfort and kindness for all whom I encounter in life."

"To learn how to use humor and kindness to help people adjust to the inevitable changes that come with aging and ill health."

> *"My alarm clock doesn't wake
> me, my purpose does."*
> —Angyil McNeal

Action Step

Continue playing with your purpose statement until something grabs you. Be gentle with yourself. Enjoy the ride.

Chapter 6
Different Approaches to Your Purpose

> *"Nothing can withstand the power of the human will if it is willing to stake its very existence to the extent of its purpose."*
> —Benjamin Disraeli

When I was in my early thirties, I needed to make a career change. I had just gone through a very painful and expensive business failure. My self-esteem was at a low ebb—something akin to a dead rat. Being broke wouldn't have been all that bad. It's just that with my personally secured business debts, I had whistled right on by broke.

Even so, I was determined to find some meaning and start a new career. I had no clue what that was. And I knew that my need for income—I had four children at the time—was going to be a driving force in any choices I was going to make.

I wanted to find my purpose, but I needed a job even more.

To take the financial needs out of the equation as much as possible, I decided to play a game. I pretended that I had won the lottery—a big one. And I tried to visualize what it would be like to have bought all the toys, cars, houses and whatever the sudden influx of wealth brought me.

What would I do then? I couldn't see myself just playing for the rest of my life. With no reason to have to work for a living, what would I *do* with my life?

Without fully realizing it, I was starting to discover my purpose. And taking the money out of the equation seemed to help.

I'm guessing that quite a few people reading this book have similar issues with money needs and may find it difficult to get to their real purpose because of it.

If so, I invite you to envision for yourself what you would do if you didn't *need* to do anything. It's kind of a fun process, actually.

I'm confident that if you truly want to live your best life, the *things* in life—as fun and as cool as they might be—will eventually be unfulfilling. I'm all for having fun, but I don't think many people will find having fun to be their purpose.

I firmly believe that you can earn a good living—even become very wealthy—by fulfilling your purpose. It might not happen quickly, and you may have to make some compromises initially, but your purpose can be profitable. Your avocation can be your vocation. I've done it and many others have as well. More than 80 percent of what I do I would do for nothing.

Action Step

Do some journaling about what your life would be like if money was no object. What would you do for nothing? Imagine winning the lottery and a year later, maybe five, when you have bought all the stuff, taken the trips, etc., what would you spend your life doing?

My Declaration of Independence

In the spring of 1985, I resigned my position as Executive Director of a financial management firm to start a magazine. It was a bold but scary move. And I marked it by inviting my friends to a party and shared with them something I had written. It was my own personal Declaration of Independence. I share it with you because it helped me at a time of change and uncertainty to stay true to my purpose.

I, Michael E. Angier, child of the Universe, in order to form a more perfect union with God, establish prosperity and well-being and insure integrity, declare myself free and independent from all bondage— past, present and future.

I divorce myself from self-righteousness, impatience, control and need for attention. I release myself from poverty, lack and negativity.

I break free from judgment and comparing myself to others, from acts of dependency and being cool;, from self-denial, indecision and timidity. I release myself from fear, worry, dishonesty, reaction and resentment.

Michael E. Angier

I remove myself from working just for money and false security and commit myself to adding value and making my heart sing in everything I do.

I ask my friends to be truthful in telling me of any times they see me fall back into any of these old patterns, which no longer serve me.

I, Michael E. Angier, co-creator of my world, dedicate myself to personal mastery, success, honesty, joy, fun and adventure. I center myself in the flow of truth, wisdom and inspiration and I choose perfect health, energy and vitality. I forgive myself and others for all mistakes. I am grateful and appreciative for all the richness in my life. I allow myself to be vulnerable and at risk. I am open and receptive to the wisdom and intelligence of the Universe.

I am free and independent. I choose love and therefore life.

—Michael E. Angier

I still have the original document signed by me and nearly 20 of my friends.

Action Step

If this type of exercise in commitment speaks to you, I encourage you to make your own declaration to help you stay on purpose.

Chapter 7
Digging Deeper

"He who has a why to live for
can bear almost any how."
—Friedrich Nietzsche

Seven Levels Deep

This exercise is used by American consultant Joe Stump with his high-level clients. The idea of Seven Levels Deep is to ask seven consecutive questions. Each question leads to the next, but you have to do it seven times. The purpose is to get to the real reasons and get down to the core of what truly motivates us.

Joe recommends that you do this exercise more than once because different times, different moods and even different places will produce different results. He also recommends that you engage the help of someone to ask the questions rather than trying to do it by yourself—although it can be done alone.

This is an empowering exercise and can make a profound difference in your purpose being deeper, more real and more meaningful to you. It's also a great way to test your confidence in your selected purpose. It might even cause you to go back to the drawing board if you're not satisfied with your answers.

Dean Graziosi hired Joe to help him promote his book, *Millionaire Success Habits*, and Joe did this exercise with him to understand Dean's real why for writing the book. It's a good example of the process that *you* might start with the question, "Why is this your purpose?"

It went like this:

Why did you write this book, Dean?

To change a million lives by helping them see a better path and better habits to success.

Why do you want to change a million lives?

Because it feels amazing to serve and help others.

Why does it feel amazing to serve and help others?

It allows for an even more successful business based on solid principles and values.

Why is it important for you to have a business based on principles and values?

I want to leave a legacy my family will be proud of.

Why is it important to leave a legacy for your family?

I never wanted to go backwards. Hated being broke as a kid.

Why do you never want to go backward?

I want my kids to have choices as they grow up.

Why is it important for your kids to have choices that you never had?

Because I want to be in control. I want to live life on my terms and be free to do as I choose.

The whole idea is to get past the head answers and get to the heart answers.

A clear and Empowering Purpose is a great thing. But knowing your WHY for the purpose is what will fuel you through the inevitable challenges you will face. You will go forward with determination, high resolve, confidence and resilience.

Action Step

Enroll a trusted friend and go through the Seven Levels Deep exercise starting with the question, "Why is your purpose of _____ important to you?"

Michael E. Angier

Chapter 8
Your Purpose May Be Bigger than You Think

"Efforts and courage are not enough without purpose and direction."
—John F. Kennedy

I have great admiration and respect for Buckminster "Bucky" Fuller. He's probably best known as an architect who designed the Geodesic Dome, the Dymaxion House and many others. But I think he will be best known as a philosopher.

Although he once went without speaking for two years, this brilliant man would talk for hours in paragraph-long sentences that were difficult to decipher. But when their meaning became clearer, his wisdom and insight was remarkably evident.

I've never argued with anything he wrote or said. But one thing he said really did bother me—for a while. And it might you if you are committed to uncovering your Empowering Purpose.

What I heard him say was, "Your true purpose will forever remain obscure."

Michael E. Angier

"Your true purpose will forever remain obscure"
—Buckminster Fuller

And it really did bother me. Because I truly wanted to know my purpose. The worst thing I could imagine was lying on my death bed not knowing what my purpose was—that I had wasted my life. It gnawed at me for several years.

Was he right? What I eventually came to understand was the context in which he'd said it. And this awareness freed me from my nagging discomfort.

I believe that what he meant is that we are all most likely involved in a much higher purpose than we are capable of understanding. Just as the bumblebee who is going after nectar in the flower is actually fulfilling a higher purpose (unbeknownst to it) of pollenating flowers.

So just as we are embarked on our purpose—as important and meaningful as we think it is—we may very well be fulfilling a much higher purpose that we can't even begin to fathom.

Whether this premise is true or not, we will likely never know.

The important thing is to know and be in the service of your Empowering Purpose.

Think about it. If Christopher Columbus hadn't been sailing west to get to India, he would not have run into and "discovered" the North American continent. So good things come from taking action—even if they weren't the intended outcome.

I still believe it's important to uncover and live into your Empowering Purpose. It certainly makes for a more interesting, meaningful and significant life. And who knows; it may even be a higher purpose than you realize.

Michael E. Angier

Chapter 9
Clarity Leads to Power

---

*"Success is a product of
unremitting attention
to purpose."*
—Benjamin Disraeli

I've spent most of my adult life studying what works and what doesn't when it comes to living a best life. One of the things I've found that separates the successful from the non-successful is *clarity*. Winners know what they want, why they want it and have plans to get it. They are clear on their principles, clear on their strategies and rarely give up. I'm sure you're not surprised by that.

The whole purpose of this book series is to help you get clear on your Core Values, your Empowering Purpose, your Meaningful Mission and your Vivid Vision. From this solid foundation, you can effectively and wisely choose the goals, projects and tasks that will create your Best Life.

What I've found is that knowing yourself well, and having the clarity to this path of success, places you in the best position to win.

Always look for the truth. Stay focused on things that matter. Rout out confusion with clarity. Ask the tough questions. Seek solutions. Challenge your beliefs.

I look at beliefs as strongly held opinions or conclusions. They are not "right" or "wrong"; they are either empowering or *dis*empowering.

And I feel confident that as you uncover and discover your Empowering Purpose, along with the other foundational building blocks of Core Values, Mission and Vision, you will continue to gain clarity and wisdom.

Action Step

I'm always glad to hear from readers as to how these ideas have helped them in their quest for their Best Life. Drop me a quick note about your insights, breakthroughs and discernments. I promise to read them. Email me at BeYourBest@SuccessNet.org

Chapter 10
Overcoming Challenges to Your Purpose

---

*"Success demands singleness
of purpose."*
—Vince Lombardi

I think it's important to know the pitfalls, the distractions and the enemies of developing your Empowering Purpose. In knowing them, you are better equipped to fight them off or avoid them.

Here's what I see as the most common challenges to uncovering and living your Empowering Purpose.

Thinking Too Small

Small goals are easier to believe in, but they lack motivation. A small goal says, you can have me any time you want. But "any time" often becomes "no time" because it's insufficiently inspiring. What's easy to do is easy *not* to do.

Make sure your Empowering Purpose is big enough and worthy enough of your best efforts. Otherwise you will be cheating yourself—big time!

Lack of Belief

You have to believe in yourself, in your purpose, your mission, your vision—and in the power of this whole process.

53

Michael E. Angier

Creating your Empowering Purpose using the strategies and tactics I've shared with you is not theoretical. These strategies have worked for many people, and they will work for you.

Invisible Purpose

One of the things that will take you off track is not keeping your Empowering Purpose front and center in your life. Out of sight is very often out of mind.

Review it often. Keep reminders of the various aspects of your Purpose. See The Best Life Navigator below.

But bear in mind that forgetting about your Purpose can happen. Life gets busy and you can find yourself majoring in minor things.

Avoid the Nay' Sayers

Not everyone you encounter is going to be supportive and encouraging about your Empowering Purpose.

Be very careful who you share it with because even well-intentioned people can throw cold water on your dreams—oftentimes in the name of being *realistic*. If you're serious about living a big life, you can't spend time with small-thinking people. You simply can't afford it.

Best Life Navigator

I created a template for Microsoft OneNote as a way to keep all my personal development, ideas, goals, core values, purpose, mission and vision statements, etc., all in one place.

It's called The Best Life Navigator™ and it really pulls everything together nicely. It's like a dashboard for living your best life. The Best Life Navigator will keep you much more organized, focused and directed.

As a reader of this book, you can get 50% off the current price when you use the coupon code PURPOSE. It comes with three valuable bonuses that I'm sure you will find useful. Full details at . . .

www.BestLifeNavigator.com

The main thing to keep in mind is to have your Empowering Purpose be a constant and uplifting reminder of the life you are choosing to live—and the reason for doing so.

Michael E. Angier

Chapter 11
The Path to Your Best Life

"Definiteness of purpose is the starting point of all achievement."
—W. Clement Stone

As you saw from the Path to Your Best Life graphic in Chapter One, there are three other foundational aspects to living your Best Life.

They are your Core Values, your Mission and your Vivid Vision.

I'm writing at least two more books in this series to address these very important topics. See Other Books by Michael Angier at the end of this book.

The reason is that your Empowering Purpose will be better and more complete if you are clear on your core values and the mission and vision for your life.

John Maxwell said, "Your core values are the deeply held beliefs that authentically describe your soul." And Stephen Covey said, "How different our lives are when we really know what is deeply important to us, and, keeping that picture in mind, we manage ourselves each day to be and to know what really matters most."

Michael E. Angier

I believe both of these wise men.

And at www.YourCoreValues.com I share the *Top Ten Reasons to Know and Live Your Core Values.*

Also on that site, you can get discounted access to a home-study course that goes in-depth into how to discover, document, articulate and live your core values. It's also available in a video course as part of the home-study course at no additional cost.

Action Step

For ideas, insight and tips on how to create a meaningful Mission Statement, go to www.SuccessNet.org/mission. It's a Smart Guide on how to create your Motivating Mission Statement, and I've made it available to you at no cost.

Chapter 12
In Summary

"The purpose of life is not to be happy. It is to be useful, to be honorable, to be compassionate, to have it make some difference that you have lived and lived well."
—Ralph Waldo Emerson

As important as having a clear and Empowering Purpose for your life is, I also believe you should enjoy the journey. You can and should be happy as you construct this beautiful life of yours—even when it's trying and challenging.

I love what my mentor Jim Rohn had to say about this: "Learn how to be happy with what you have, while you pursue all that you want."

"Learn how to be happy with what you have, while you pursue all that you want."
—Jim Rohn

One more word about not getting too quickly involved in the *how* of living your Empowering Purpose. Getting too attached to the *way* your purpose will be fulfilled limits the manner in which it will be achieved. Focus on the results, not the path.

How Did We Do?

I began planning and writing this book with several objectives.

> 1. Convince you of the value and the wisdom of investing in the discovery and development of an Empowering Purpose for your life.

> 2. Help you to think bigger and believe in the possibilities of living up to your full and unique potential.

> 3. Encourage you to believe more in yourself, in this process and in what's possible.

> 4. Share resources and recommendations that will help you to create a clear and Empowering Purpose as a guiding light for living your Best Life.

> 5. Help you to dig deeper, think more comprehensively and eventually live in a more balanced, meaningful and significant fashion.

I hope we've been able to accomplish this together.

And if your Empowering Purpose is not yet clear to you, then that's your mission for now—to find your purpose.

I wish for you to know your Empowering Purpose, have a Meaningful Mission, live your Vivid Vision, accomplish great things and feel the happiness, fulfillment and satisfaction that comes from a life well lived.

You can do it! And you deserve it!

Have fun!

A Thank You and a Request

Thank you for reading my book! I really appreciate all of your feedback, and I love hearing what you have to say.

I need your input to make the next version of this book— and my future books—better.

Please leave a brief and helpful review on Amazon to let me know what you thought of the book. Only about one in a thousand readers leave a review. I hope you will be a one-in-a-thousand reader.

You can use this link:
www.SuccessNet.org/go/amz-author

Thank you very much.

Michael E. Angier

BeYourBest@SuccessNet.org
www.SuccessNet.org

About the Author

Michael E. Angier is the founder and CIO (Chief Inspiration Officer) of SuccessNet based in the Tampa Bay area of Florida. He's a father, grandfather, husband, writer, speaker, entrepreneur, coach and student.

He's the author of the *101 Best Ways series, The Achievement Code, The Secret to Being Fiercely Focused, How to Create a Vivid Vision for Your Life* and others.

Michael's work has been featured in numerous publications such as *USA Today, Selling Power, Personal Excellence* and *Sales & Marketing Excellence* as well as dozens of electronic publications. He's been interviewed on both TV and radio many times.

And his internationally popular articles have earned him a Paul Harris Fellowship with Rotary International.

Angier has experienced personal and professional success, but he's also suffered some bitter defeats. Although certainly preferring the former, he feels that he's learned the most from his struggles and disappointments. He feels that life's greatest lessons are learned by overcoming the obstacles in the path of a challenging and worthwhile objective.

Michael E. Angier

Michael's passion is human potential. He believes fervently in the indomitable human spirit and revels in helping people and companies grow and prosper.

Over the past 40 years, Michael has devoted himself to studying what works and has been an ardent student of the principles of success. He's taught seminars and conducted workshops on goal setting, motivation and personal development in six countries.

Michael feels that there are three things essential to living a fulfilling and successful life: a purpose to live for, a self to live with and a faith to live by.

Michael is married to Dawn Angier—his partner, best friend, mentor, teacher, student and confidante. They have six adult children and five grandchildren. Michael enjoys tennis, reading, writing, publishing and helping people realize their dreams.

Mistakes Happen

We're committed to publishing inspiring, practical and professional books. However, mistakes do occur. If you should find a typographical, grammatical or factual error, we would be most grateful if you let us know. And, if you are the first to tell us about it, we'd be happy to send you a thank you gift.

Just email your find with the book name, location and type of error to BeYourBest@SuccessNet.org with "Found This!" in the subject. Thanks for your help.

Other Books by Michael Angier
www.Amazon.com/author/michaelangier

The Achievement Code
The 3C Formula for Getting What You Truly Want

The Achievement Code offers a simple, but proven, formula for getting what you truly want. With the Three C's, the author has distilled down from both ancient and modern teachers the true alchemy of success and achievement.

Whether they realized it or not, every single person who has ever achieved great things has employed the Three-C Formula. But not until Angier identified the Three Cs did the formula reveal itself. *The Achievement Code* outlines in simple, straightforward steps how to practice Clarity, Concentration and Consistency and actually get what you really want. Best-selling author, Bob Burg, writes in the Foreword, "It contains the basic principles of success upon which Michael has built his own ultra-successful life and business and upon which anyone else can do the same. In these teachings, he lays the foundation from which anyone can decide on a certain goal and by the very nature of the instruction provided, go about achieving it.

Other Books by Michael Angier

www.Amazon.com/author/michaelangier

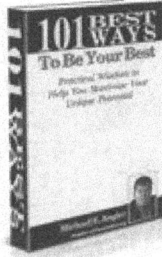

101 Best Ways to Be Your Best
Practical Wisdom to Help You Maximize
Your Unique Potential

This book offers practical advice and motivates you on a quest for your best.

Through easy-to-read stories and passages, Michael reveals:

- What a simple tennis game can teach you about goal setting
- The vital importance of thankfulness
- How setting clear intentions increases your chance of hitting your mark
- Why worrying is counterproductive to achieving your goals
- And much, much more . . .

Michael E. Angier

Other Books by Michael Angier
www.Amazon.com/author/michaelangier

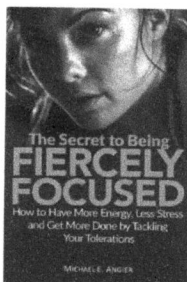

The Secret to Being Fiercely Focused

How to Have More Energy, Less Stress and
Get More Done by Tackling Your Tolerations.

Are You Ready to Declutter Your Mind?

The Life-Changing Magic of Tidying Up: The Japanese Art of Decluttering and Organizing, has been off and on the New York Times Best Seller list for years—mostly on. If decluttering your home and office is life-changing, what about decluttering your *mind?*

Hundreds of thousands of books have been written on success—about what you need to get ahead. But what isn't talked about much is *what you need to get rid of.*

These spirit-sucking, energy-draining, peace-killers steal our joy, our happiness, our energy and our focus.

They are called Tolerations—things we tolerate, but shouldn't. And like weeds in a garden, we must recognize them for what they are and hoe them out—or they will take over our garden (life).

68

Other Books by Michael Angier

www.Amazon.com/author/michaelangier

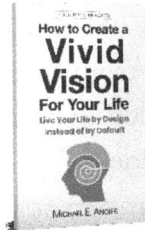

Do You Have a Clear Vision for Your Life?

How to Create a Vivid Vision for Your Life gives you the impetus, the tools and the guidelines to create a meaningful, inspiring and detailed vision for your best life.

The author takes you by the hand and helps you dream big, think big and act even bigger.

This book will help you to . . .

- create a clear picture of the life you wish to create
- have more clarity and direction
- make better decisions and make them more easily
- have more balance in your life
- have more meaning and significance
- be more inspired, focused and motivated
- have more happiness by living on your terms

Don't let another day go by without creating a Vivid Vision for Your Life. Get your copy of this book now and make the rest of your life the best of your life.

Free Resources

Personal Achievement Assessment

Download this free tool from SuccessNet. With it, you'll be able to evaluate yourself in many different areas of your life and find even more ideas for living your Empowering Purpose. Consider it your personal success inventory (PDF format).
www.SuccessNet.org/psa

Report: Raising the Bar

Increase your standards of excellence. Your special report may be downloaded at
www.SuccessNet.org/files/raisethebar.pdf

Strengths/Talents/Knowledge/Skills List

Helping You to Identify Your Zone of Genius
www.SuccessNet.org/mission/genius.pdf

Dedication

This book is dedicated to my six children: Michael, Michelle, Sarah, Bradford, Kevin and Will. They are now all adults making their own way through their lives.

They are all different from one another and are each embarked on different career paths.

They have very much enriched my life and I am truly grateful for what they have taught me. I was not always there for them at every turn. And I certainly was not the Poster Dad for best father.

But I've come to believe that the only real mistake a parent can make is for their children to not get that you love them. And love them I do. I'm sure they know this. I'm very proud of each of them.

And it's heartwarming to know they are living purposeful, meaningful and significant lives. If I've played any role in inspiring them or helping them do that, then I feel content and fulfilled.

It's sometimes hard to tell how much influence you've had on someone, and I'm fortunate to have been told by most of them that I have. It's gratifying indeed.

Michael E. Angier

Acknowledgements

I am truly grateful for my wife, Dawn, who is my business and life partner as well as my best friend. She provided not only encouragement and feedback, but also her highly professional copy editing and technical expertise. She always makes me—and my work—look better.

In addition, I wish to thank the tens of thousands of subscribers and members of SuccessNet, who over the past 24 years, have followed me and supported our efforts in helping us all create and live our Best Lives. They—and you—are a great source of inspiration to me. And your patronage has allowed me to do work that I love for over two decades.

Made in USA - Kendallville, IN
1058935_9781076439307
03.20.2020 1605